MY WELLBEING JOURNAL

WAVERLEY ABBEY
RESOURCES

Published 2019 by Waverley Abbey Resources, Waverley Abbey House, Waverley Lane, Farnham,
Surrey GU9 8EP, UK. Waverley Abbey Resources is an operating name of CWR.

Registered Charity No. 294387. Registered Limited Company No. 1990308.

Reprinted 2022.

For a list of National Distributors, visit waverleyabbeyresources.org/distributors

Scripture references are taken from: Holy Bible, New International Version® Anglicized, NIV®
Copyright © 1979, 1984, 2011 by Biblica, Inc.® Used by permission. All rights reserved worldwide.
Other versions are marked: Holy Bible, New Living Translation, copyright © 1996, 2004, 2015 by
Tyndale House Foundation. Used by permission of Tyndale House Publishers, Inc., Carol Stream,
Illinois 60188. All rights reserved. The Message. Copyright © 1993, 1994, 1995, 1996, 2000, 2001,
2002. Used by permission of NavPress Publishing Group.

Multiple references taken from Patrick Regan with Liz Hoeksma, Honesty Over Silence
(Waverley Abbey Resources, 2019)

Concept development, editing, design and production by Waverley Abbey Resources.

Every effort has been made to ensure that this book contains the correct permissions and
references, but if anything has been inadvertently overlooked the Publisher will be pleased to
make the necessary arrangements at the first opportunity. Please contact the Publisher directly.

Printed in the UK by Page Bros

ISBN: 978-1-78951-148-2

Introduction

I have been journalling for 20 years now and I can honestly say that it has been a lifeline for me. Although I don't tend to write in my journal every day, I normally do so twice a week. I write down things that have happened to me, as well as my thoughts and feelings. I also write about some of the amazing people I meet and the lessons they teach me. When travelling, I tend to journal every day as I want to remember the experiences I am having and what I am learning.

As I write, I get some of the thoughts that seem to be stuck on repeat in my head down on paper, and I recognise that not everything I think is true. The thing I particularly love about journalling is that, as I am the only one who reads my journal, I am released from the fear of being judged by others. Although I think it's important for us all to be honest and share our journeys through telling our stories, I love and cherish the moments when I have the space and time to write honestly through journalling, as in those moments I can be completely real because it's just me and God. This isn't filtered; this is me.

The books I read also have an impact on the way I journal. When I read, I underline what speaks to me personally and copy it down. The wisdom I capture from those who have written and thought things through before me is amazing, and I don't want to lose those words that have so many times spoken straight into my situation. I will never have the time to pick up ten books to look back on and find all the things that impacted me, but I can easily pick up my journal. Then, once a month, I try to sit down and glance back over the last three months' entries in my journal. As I do this, I'm encouraged about all the good that I have experienced in my life, big and small, and I'm also reminded of the love of God through the pages that speak of hope even in my bleakest moments.

God is not scared of my honesty; He doesn't mind me expressing my frustration. God's people have done so from time immemorial, as is evident throughout the Bible. You only have to read Psalms and see David crying out to God expressing feelings of anger, despair, frustration and anxiety to realise this. Like me, David had so many questions and faced so much uncertainty. In fact, many of the psalms are laments – honest cries out to God. When I feel like I'm facing darkness and am struggling to pray, I find it helpful to write letters to God in my journal. Some are very raw and direct. I find myself asking God, 'What is going on?' I don't understand why certain things happen to me, and I don't understand the pain I see in the world around me, but I know I that I can express these feelings to Him.

It is one of those dark times many years ago, when I went into hospital for major limb reconstruction surgery, that changed the direction of both my life and the life of my family. I had been so scared to have the operation and the effect it would have on my family that I put it off for six years until eventually the pain in my body meant I couldn't put it off anymore. Before I walked into the hospital, knowing that I wouldn't be able to walk properly for a long time afterwards, I wrote these words:

Hope – what is it?

Hope is knowing there is a bigger picture; hope is the realisation that I am never alone.

Hope is knowing that all the thousands of thoughts that confuse me make perfect sense to the one who made me.

Hope is seeing beyond what we are now and seeing what we can become.

Hope is knowing that true love is the most powerful force on earth.

Hope is knowing that change is possible when we listen to life's whispers along our way.

Hope is the restoration of everything that get stolen: joy, health, laughter.

In this journal, you'll find quotes to inspire you and make you think – from people throughout history, the Bible and *Honesty Over Silence* written by myself with Liza Hoeksma.
 I hope that using this journal in both the good times and the challenging times will be a real encouragement to you and a constant reminder that you are loved and valuable, and that there is hope.

Patrick Regan OBE
Co-Founder and CEO of Kintsugi Hope

It's OK
not to be OK.

Today...

The LORD is my rock,
my fortress, and my savior;
my God is my rock, in whom
I find protection. He is my
shield, the power that saves
me, and my place of safety.

Today...

I am half agony,
half hope.

JANE AUSTEN, *PERSUASION*

Today...

Ordinary riches can be stolen,
real riches cannot. In your soul
are infinitely precious things
that cannot be taken from you.

OSCAR WILDE

Today...

We belong
to someone who
loves us.

SELWYN HUGHES

Today...

In His incredible love, God will make something even more beautiful out of the broken parts of our lives – if we allow Him to.

Today...

LOVE...

always protects,

always trusts,

always hopes,

always perseveres.

1 CORINTHIANS 13:6–7

Today...

Flawsome: *adjective.*
When a person knows they are
awesome, despite their flaws.

Today...

We don't get to choose
when darkness comes
into our lives, and we
will all face it sooner
or later. The choice
we have is whether or
not we engage with
the darkness, knowing
that God meets us
right there in our pain.

Today...

Integrity is telling
myself the truth.

And honesty is
telling the truth
to other people.

SPENCER JOHNSON

Today...

*Wanting to be someone else
is a waste
of the person you are.*

MARILYN MONROE

Today...

Are you tired? Worn out?
Burned out on religion?
Come to me. Get away with
me and you'll recover your
life. I'll show you how to take
a real rest. Walk with me and
work with me—watch how
I do it. Learn the unforced
rhythms of grace. I won't lay
anything heavy or ill-fitting
on you. Keep company with
me and you'll learn to live
freely and lightly.

JESUS CHRIST (MATTHEW 11:28–30, *THE MESSAGE*)

Today...

_____

_____

_____

_____

_____

_____

_____

_____

_____

_____

_____

_____

_____

_____

_____

_____

_____

This painful, broken place is a beautiful and bountiful opportunity for blessing.

RACHEL WRIGHT

Tim and Rachel Wright, *Shattered* (Waverley Abbey Resources, 2019)

Today...

A thought is harmless
unless we believe it.

BYRON KATIE

Loving What Is: Four Questions That Can Change Your Life (New York: Harmony Books, 2003)

Today...

Refuse to be average.
Let your heart
soar
as high as it will.

A.W. TOZER

Today...

HE GIVES POWER
TO THE WEAK AND
STRENGTH TO
THE POWERLESS.

ISAIAH 40:29, NLT

Today...

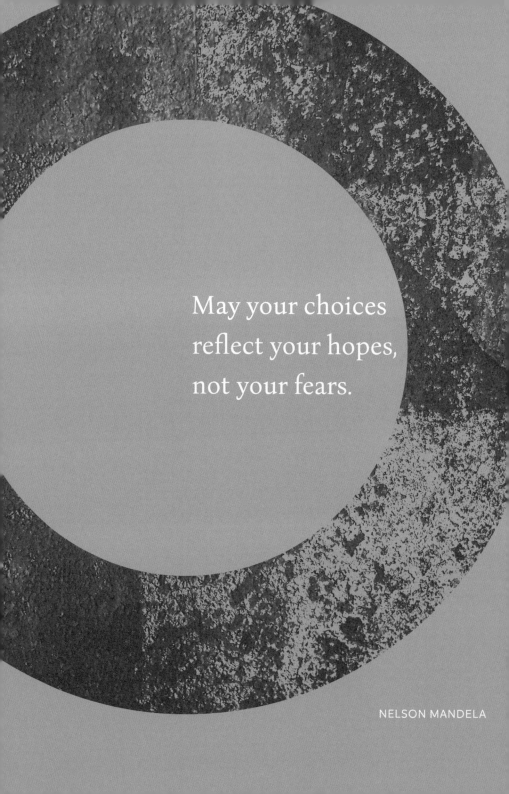

May your choices
reflect your hopes,
not your fears.

NELSON MANDELA

Today...

Be still

PSALM 46:10

Today...

We are all broken, but owning our
story is one way we step out of shame.

Today...

God

loves each of us
as if there were
only one
of us.

Today...

whatever is true, whatever is noble,
whatever is right, whatever is pure,
whatever is lovely, whatever is
admirable – if anything is excellent
or praiseworthy – think about
such things.

PHILIPPIANS 4:8

Today...

Be kind,

for everyone you meet is fighting a hard battle.

SOCRATES

Today...

_____

_____

_____

_____

_____

_____

_____

_____

_____

_____

_____

_____

_____

_____

_____

_____

_____

but those who wait on the LORD shall renew their strength. They will soar on wings like eagles; they will run and not grow weary, they will walk and not be faint.

Today...

You are imperfect,
permanently and
inevitably flawed.
And you are
beautiful.

AMY BLOOM

Today...

_____

_____

_____

_____

_____

_____

_____

_____

_____

_____

_____

_____

_____

_____

_____

_____

_____

_____

_____

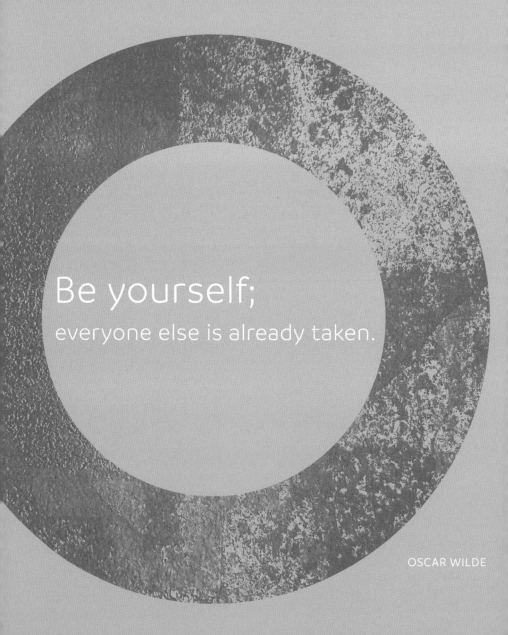

Be yourself;
everyone else is already taken.

OSCAR WILDE

Today...

Who you become
while you are
waiting is as
important as what
you are waiting for.

Today...

My grace is sufficient for you, for my power is made perfect in weakness.

2 CORINTHIANS 12:9

Today...

NO ONE CAN MAKE YOU FEEL INFERIOR WITHOUT YOUR CONSENT.

ELEANOR ROOSEVELT

Today...

We must accept finite disappointment, but never lose infinite

HOPE.

Today...

Courage isn't having the
strength to go on –
it is going on when
you don't have strength.

NAPOLÉON BONAPARTE

Today...

The fundamental fact of existence is that this trust in God, this faith, is the firm foundation under everything that makes life worth living. It's our handle on what we can't see.

HEBREWS 11:1–2, *THE MESSAGE*

Today...

We need to learn to *celebrate* the small steps in life.

Today...

Speak what we feel,
not what we
ought to say.

SHAKESPEARE, *KING LEAR*

Today...

Cast all your
anxiety on
him because
he cares for
you.

1 PETER 5:7

Today...

Hope is the thing with feathers

That perches in the soul,

And sings the tune without the words,

And never stops at all

EMILY DICKINSON

Today...

Other people are going to
find healing in your wounds.
Your greatest life messages
and your most effective
ministry will come out of
your deepest hurts.

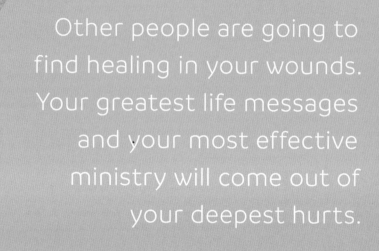

RICK WARREN
Purpose Driven Life (Grand Rapids: Zondervan, 2002)

Today...

An honest answer is like a kiss on the lips.

Today...

Often we are so focused on
the destination that we forget
that God is more concerned
with the state of our hearts as
we journey towards it.

Today...

*In the middle of a difficulty
lies opportunity.*

ALBERT EINSTEIN

Today...

He heals the
broken-hearted
and binds up
their wounds.

PSALM 147:3

Today...

Waiting reminds us we are not in control, and we can't command things to happen on a schedule that suits us. Sometimes we need to let go of our own plans and ideas. We need to stop rushing and just wait a while, listening to God's whisper.

Today...

to thine own self be true

SHAKESPEARE, *HAMLET*

Today...

But God demonstrates
his own love for us in this:
while we were still sinners,
Christ died for us.

Today...

One of the most prominent lies... is that

our lives are a reflection of God's feelings

towards us at that moment. In other words,

if my world is going well, then God is pleased

with me; if I am facing a challenge, then God

is angry... or at the very least, disappointed.

This is simply not true.

JEN BAKER

Unshakeable Confidence (Waverley Abbey Resources, 2008)

Today...

It's actually healthy to express
our pain, anger and fear...
God is with us and loves us
no matter what's going on.

Today...

I have not failed.
I've just found
10,000 ways
that won't work.

THOMAS EDISON

Today...

'they will call him Immanuel'
(which means 'God with us').

MATTHEW 1:23

Today...

We need to stop and remember that
we are treasures in the hands of God.
He has scooped us up with our cracks
and chips. He holds us, and even
when others might pass us by
without a glance, He says,
'You are mine. You are treasured.'

TIM WRIGHT

Rachel and Tim Wright, *Shattered* (Waverley Abbey Resources, 2019)

Today...

When we let go of the unrealistic image of who we think we're supposed to be, we can get on with being the unique person God created us to be.

Today...

To be yourself in a world that is constantly trying to make you something else is the greatest accomplishment.

RALPH WALDO EMERSON

Today...

I can do all this through him who gives me **strength.**

PHILIPPIANS 4:13

Today...

I'm not afraid
of storms,
for I'm learning
how to
sail my ship.

Today...

You may not control all the events that happen to you, but you can decide not to be reduced by them.

MAYA ANGELOU
Letter to My Daughter (London: Random House, 2008)

Today...

We are loved, enjoyed
and liked by God.
We need to build a
resilience that allows
us to listen to other
people's approval and
criticism of us without
letting it define us.

Today...

I believe we need to let go of the harmful notion that there are 'those in need' and 'those able to help'. We are all in need in some way, and we can all help others.

Today...

Out of your
vulnerabilities
will come
your strength,

SIGMUND FREUD

Today...

You are fearfully and wonderfully made by Almighty God, and He thinks you're worth dying for.

Today...

Experience is not what happens to you. It is what you do with what happens to you. Don't waste your pain; use it to help others.

Purpose Driven Life (Grand Rapids: Zondervan, 2002)

Today...

I am convinced that neither death nor life,
neither angels nor demons, neither the
present nor the future, nor any powers,
neither height nor depth, nor anything
else in all creation, will be able to separate
us from the love of God

ROMANS 8:38–39

Today...

only when it is dark enough
can you see the stars.

MARTIN LUTHER KING JR.

Today...

There is no limit
to what God
would do for us.

Today...

The light shines in the darkness,
and the darkness has not
overcome it.

JOHN 1:5

Today...

Suffering has been stronger than all other teaching, and has taught me to understand what your heart used to be. I have been bent and broken, but – I hope – into a better shape.

CHARLES DICKENS, *GREAT EXPECTATIONS*

Today...

I want
my weakness
to reveal
a strong
God.

Today...

I am certain
that God,
who began
the good
work within
you, will
continue
his work
until it
is finally
finished

PHILIPPIANS 1:6, NLT

Today...

We delight in the beauty of the butterfly, but rarely admit the changes it has gone through to achieve that beauty.

MAYA ANGELOU

Today...

The more we know who God is and who He says we are, the easier we will find it to hold on to the truth and let the lies go.

Today...

_____

_____

_____

_____

_____

_____

_____

_____

_____

_____

_____

_____

_____

_____

_____

_____

_____

_____

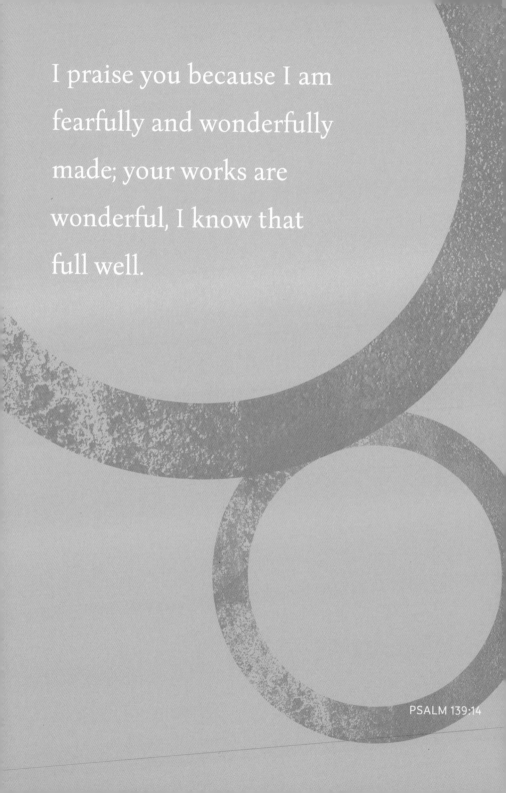

I praise you because I am
fearfully and wonderfully
made; your works are
wonderful, I know that
full well.

PSALM 139:14

Today...

It is never too late
to be
what you might have been.

GEORGE ELIOT

Today...

Your attitude about who you are and what you have is a very little thing that makes a very big difference.

THEODORE ROOSEVELT

Today...

_____

_____

_____

_____

_____

_____

_____

_____

_____

_____

_____

_____

_____

_____

_____

_____

We are free to express
everything we're feeling before
a God who knows and loves us.

Today...

Acceptance in the anguish
Beauty in the bruises
Belief in the brokenness
Breakthrough in the battle
Comfort in the conflict
Contentment in the confusion
Courage in the crisis
Determination in the distress
Diamonds in the dust
Dignity in the disappointment
Direction in the difficulty
Discovery in the darkness
Faith in the fear
Fortitude in the frustration
Grace in the grief
Healing in the horror
Hope in the hurt
Insight in the injury
Inspiration in the illness

Lessons in the living
Love in the loneliness
Mercy in the misunderstanding
Opportunity in the ordeal
Patience in the problems
Peace in the panic
Perseverance in the perplexity
Purpose in the pain
Refuge in the regrets
Rest in the restrictions
Sanctuary in the suffering
Serenity in the scars
Shelter in the shock
Stillness in the storm
Strength in the shadows
Support in the sadness
Treasure in the trials
Trust in the trauma
Victory in the vulnerability
Wisdom in the weakness

JANE SMITH

Today...

_____

_____

_____

_____

_____

_____

_____

_____

_____

_____

_____

_____

_____

_____

_____

_____

_____

Rejoice in our
confident hope.
Be patient in trouble,
and keep on praying.

ROMANS 12:12, NLT

Today...

It is during our
darkest moments
that we must focus
to see the light.

ARISTOTLE

Today...

We need never
be ashamed of
our tears.

CHARLES DICKENS, *GREAT EXPECTATIONS*

Today...

Never, never, never give in!

WINSTON CHURCHILL

Today...

When you

pass through

the waters,

I will be

with you

ISAIAH 43:2

Today...

COURAGE IS KNOWING WHAT NOT TO FEAR.

PLATO

Today...

Honesty is the first chapter
in the book of wisdom

Today...

Be comforted, dear soul! There is always light behind the clouds.

LOUISA MAY ALCOTT, *LITTLE WOMEN*

Today...

The LORD is close to the broken-hearted and saves those who are crushed in spirit.

PSALM 34:18

Today...

_____

_____

_____

_____

_____

_____

_____

_____

_____

_____

_____

_____

_____

_____

_____

_____

_____

_____

_____

Today...

Today...

Kintsugi Hope is a charity founded by Patrick and Diane Regan, which longs to bring a message of hope for all those struggling, and an assurance that it's OK to acknowledge that you're not OK.

The vision for Wellbeing Groups is to provide safe and supportive spaces for those who are finding life overwhelming – places where people who struggle with mental and emotional health challenges are not only accepted and understood, but are given the tools to grow and flourish in community with others.

The aim of these groups, working through the local church, is to foster an attitude of humility – not to judge, fix or rescue, but to be alongside and love one another. Groups will journey together to look at being honest with each other, how to understand and handle our emotions, build healthy relationships and grow in resilience.

To find out more about the work of Kintsugi Hope and the Wellbeing Groups, visit **kintsugihope.com**

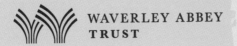
WAVERLEY ABBEY
TRUST

If you're wondering what's next for you, having enjoyed journalling with us, Waverley Abbey Trust has a wide range of books, courses and events to help you understand yourself and others, and give you insight into areas many of us struggle with in life.

Whether it's courses on counselling and pastoral care or books such as Patrick Regan's *Honesty Over Silence*, or daily Bible reading notes, we can help you to learn more about living a God-dependent life.

To find out more about what we do and how we can help, please visit **waverleyabbeytrust.org**